Python

I0004195

Arthur Keane

Introduction

I want to thank you and congratulate you for downloading the book, *"Python"*.

This book has actionable information on how to learn python programming as a beginner.

If you've been following news, you must have noted the rising number of people talking about how computer programming is the latest 'superpower' that is not being taught in many schools. Why do you think famous and successful computer programmers such as Drew Houston and Mark Zuckerberg are always pointing to computer programming when talking about the way to successfully navigate the modern technological world?

Well, it is simple; the importance of computer programming knowledge in the present day is simply indescribable. Even if you are not an IT professional, having a good understanding of programming will definitely be something to add on to your skillset, which can set you apart from many jobseekers out there. And what better way to learn programming than to start by learning a programming language like python? While there are many great programming languages out there, learning python is perhaps the one programming language that you don't want pass even if you are a beginner programmer because:

- ✓ The Python programming language is extremely easy to learn, and you can use it as a stepping stone into frameworks and other languages.

- ✓ You can use it to develop prototypes very fast since it is easy to read and work with.

✓ Most data mining, automation and large data platforms usually rely on Python mainly because it is the standard/ideal language to use for wide-ranging tasks.

✓ The language typically allows for a more productive coding environment than other massive languages such as Java and C#.

✓ The software is widely used by many people and businesses which include large companies like Instagram, Disney, Google, Yahoo!, IBM, Pinterest, Nokia and many more- and many companies are adopting it every day.

If you've decided to learn python, this book will hold you by the hand from the beginning to the very end to ensure you have all the basic details that you need to get started as programmer. By the end of this guide, you'll be able to use Python to complete tough and important projects, whether small or large very easily and more efficiently. Let's begin.

Thanks again for downloading this book. I hope you enjoy it!

The trademarks that are used are without any consent, and the publication of the trademark is without permission or backing by the trademark owner. All trademarks and brands within this book are for clarifying purposes only and are the owned by the owners themselves, not affiliated with this document.

Table of Contents

What Is Python?

Python is an object-oriented and interpreted programming language that has become increasingly popular due to its good code readability and clear syntax. When I see Python, I often think of a process of cracking a computer problem as easily as writing my thoughts out about the solution. How is that so? Well, with Python, you can write the code once and run it on nearly any computer without having to alter the program.

So how did it come into being?

Python was first conceptualized by Guido van Rossum, a smart computer programmer in 1989 when he was faced with some limitations of ABC language, specifically with regards to extensibility. He started working on developing a new language that unified all the great features of ABC language and desirable features like exception handling and extensibility.

Here is a brief summary of how python has come to become what it is today:

✓ In 1994 a series of projects and hard work saw the release of Python 1.0.

✓ Soon, the core development team of Python moved to Beopen.com to create the BeOpen PythonLabs team, just before the next Python version was released.

✓ In 2000, the BeOpen Python Labs team released Python 2.0 and the software itself contained many improvisations.

- ✓ Python 2.7, which is currently still in use was released some-time later -this constant trend depicted a development progress that so far made it clear that better software would always be released.

- ✓ In December 2008, python 3.0 was released.

- ✓ Python 3.4.3 which was released in February 2015 offered even more improvements in Unicode support, among other great, new features before Python 3.5 was then released on September the same year with more goodies.

- ✓ Today, the latest release is python 3.6 (and 3.6.1 which is the first maintenance release of python 3.6) that was released on March 2017. This version contains numerous optimizations and new features as well.

As it stands now, Python programming language remains to be the multi-paradigm language that offers developers certain options like structured programming, object orientation and functional programming.

But before we get ahead of ourselves, it is critical to understand the lingo that's in this book just to make sure you don't miss anything.

Understand The Python Lingo: Python Glossary

Every language has its lingo and if you don't have a good grasp of the terms used in a particular language, you can bet that you are likely to face problems along the way. Python is not any different; it has its lingo that you should understand if you are to really understand the language well. That's why the first thing we will mention is the lingo to ensure you don't feel lost as we discuss other aspects of the programming language. That's not all; as you read through this guide, you might find words you are not very familiar with. Please refer to this glossary when that happens:

I have included all the words I thought can be a problem to the average beginner.

Argparse- It's the parser (in simple terms, parse means analyze string symbols) for command-line options, subcommands and arguments.

Assert- A function that is used during debugging to check for conditions that should apply.

Debugging- This refers to the process of searching for and removing errors in programming.

Augment- This is the additional information that the computer uses to execute commands.

Class- This refers to a template we use to create user defined objects.

Continue- This refers to a function that is used to skip the existing block, and go back to the 'while' or 'for' statement.

Compiler-This refers to a function that we use to translate a program that is written in high-level language to a low-level language.

Conditional statement- This simply refers to a statement that has an 'if/else' or 'if'

Dictionary- The mutable associative array of value pairs and keys- it can have different types (values and keys) and the keys ought to be a hashable type.

Def- A function that defines a method or function.

Docstring- This is a string literal occurring as the initial statement in a class, module, method definition or function.

Distuitils- It's a package contained in the Python Standard Library for the installation, construction and distribution of Python code.

For- It iterates over an object while capturing all elements to a local variable to be used by the attached block.

Function- This is a parameterized series of statements.

Function call- This refers to an invocation of the function containing arguments.

Generators- This is a function that takes back an iterator.

Garbage collection- This refers to the process of releasing memory when it's no longer being used.

High-level language- A language that is made to be simple for humans to write and read.

Low-level language- This is the computer's native language- it provides slight or no abstraction from the set architecture of a computer's instruction.

Iteration- This is a process where instructions or a set of structures are repeated sequentially a particular number of times or until a specific condition is met.

Syntax- A set of rules defining how a python program is written and then interpreted.

Index- This refers to a position inside a well ordered list that's assigned to the characters – for instance, every character has an index starting from 0 to the length of -1.

Variable- This is a reserved memory location used to store values.

Script- It's the classic key module that's identified by file system path which can be executed without designation of the interpreter via the use of file association.

Break statement- When an external condition is triggered, the 'break statement' provides you the opportunity to make an exit out of a loop.

Module- This refers to an object in python that contains arbitrarily named attributes which can reference and bind. It is a file made up of Python code and can define functions, variables and classes.

Dependencies- These are visible, non-user packages containing binaries, modules or shared libraries.

Console- The place or terminal where you execute a command at a time.

Debugging- This refers to the process of identifying and removing program errors.

Instantiate- This refers to it is the process of creating an instance, which is a specific realization of a template -for example, a class of objects or a computer process.

Identifier- A name we use to identify a class, variable, module or any another object in python.

Graphical User Interface **(GUI)-** This refers to a type of interface, which enables different users to actually interact with different electronic devices through visual indicators and graphical indicators.

With that understanding, let's now get started with python starting with downloading python.

Getting Started With Python

Downloading And Installing Python

In this section, we'll discuss how to download the program on Windows and Mac OS X.

Windows

Unlike many software, Python does not come prepackaged with Windows- but this does not mean that as a Windows user you won't find this amazing language useful. In order to install the newest version properly though, we will have to make sure you get the right tools.

NOTE: Several years ago, there was an update to Python that created a significant split between the versions of Python and as a new comer, this can make things quite confusing for you, but that's not a problem; I'll walk you through the installation for the two major versions.

When you go to the python download page for Windows (https://www.python.org/downloads/windows/), you will see this division. You'll see the repository asking you whether you want the latest release of python 3 or python 2 (3.6.1 and 2.7.13 respectively).

Python Releases for Windows

- Latest Python 2 Release - Python 2.7.13
- Latest Python 3 Release - Python 3.6.1

Which one to download?

While most of us think that newer is better, the choice of version should totally depend on your end goal. For instance, say you have read some cool article about Minecraft (a popular video game) talking about how to expand a Minecraft world with MCDungeon (a map modification tool offering highly customizable way of introducing dungeons into Minecraft) and you get all excited about adding awesome stuff to your worlds. The project, coded in Python requires Python 2.7- you cannot run this particular project with Python 3.6. Actually, if you're looking to explore hobby projects such as MCDungeon, you'll realize that almost all of them use 2.7. Therefore, if your aim is getting some project which ends in 'py' extension running, there is a really good chance you'll require Python 2.7 for it.

Conversely, if you really want to focus on learning Python, I recommend you install both versions -which as you will realize, is possible with very little risk and only requiring only a small bit of setup trouble. This will let you work with the latest version of Python and also enable you run older scripts of the language (and for newer projects, test backwards compatibility). For more information about the differences between the two versions, please visit this page https://wiki.python.org/moin/Python2orPython3.

Nonetheless, if you're certain you only require a particular version, you can download either. Under the main entry for the two versions, you'll be able to see an 'x86-64' executable installer.

This installer will go ahead and install the right 64-bit or 32-bit version automatically on your computer. Don't know the difference between the two (32-bit or 64-bit

Installing python 2

Installing this version is literally a snap, and unlike in the previous years, the installer even sets the PATH variable (this variable basically specifies a set of directories where the program is located) for you. Just run the installer, choose 'install for all users' and click 'next.'

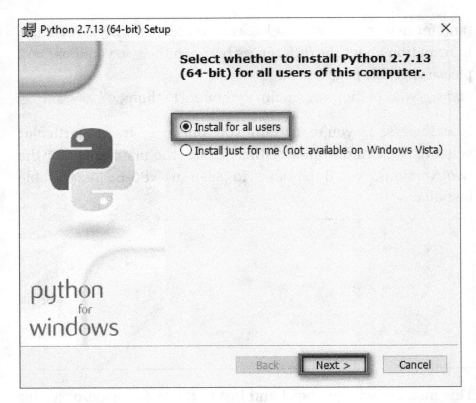

Leave the directory as 'Python27' on the directory selection screen and then click 'next.'

Scroll down on the screen and click on 'add python. exe to path,' then select 'will be installed on the local hard drive.' Click next when you're done.

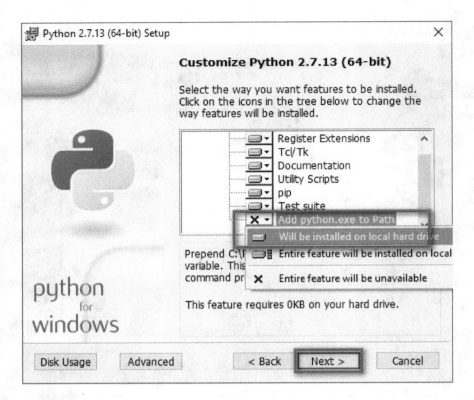

After this point, you don't really have to make any other decisions. Just ensure you click through the wizard to finish the installation. After it's complete, you can open up the command prompt to confirm the installation and type this command:

python -V

```
C:\Users\Jason>python -V
Python 2.7.13
```

Congratulations! If all you require is Python 2.7 to complete some project on Windows, your road can end here. It's now installed, and the path variable is set.

Installing Python 3

If you want to learn the latest Python version, you'll have to install Python 3. You can install it besides Python 2.7 without any trouble- so just proceed to run the executable now. On the first screen, enable the option 'add python 3.6 to PATH' and click 'install now'.

After that, you'll have an important decision to make. When you click the option- 'disable path length limit', you'll be removing the limitation on the MAX_PATH variable. This change doesn't break anything; in fact, it allows the software to use long path names. Many programmers are working in *nix systems such as Linux where the length of the path name is not an issue; thus, you can turn this on in advance to help you smooth over any issues related to path that you might encounter while working in Windows.

I suggest you go ahead and choose this option. If you know you don't want to disable the limit of the path length, you can click 'close' to complete the installation.

If you're just installing python 3, you can also use the same 'python-v" command line trick which we used above to check that it was indeed installed properly, and the path variable is set.

Mac OS X

Usually, this operating system comes with a pre-installed version of Python. For example, Mac OS X 10.8 comes with 2.7. To take advantage of the most recent versions of this program, you'll have to download and install the latest version besides the one in the system.

NOTE: You cannot rely on Python 3 to run 2.x scripts.

The steps of downloading

When you get to the Python download page, it will detect automatically that you are a user of Mac and thus offer you some options accordingly.

In no time, you'll be able to download a file containing the name 'Python 3.x.macosx10.6dmg' that heads directly into your browser's downloads folder. In case you're wondering, the 10.6 notation in the name only means that you have to at least have OS X Snow Leopard to run this file.

When you open the downloaded file, it automatically mounts as a volume on your desktop. Open the file or DMG (Disk Image) and wait to see a window similar to the one below.

NOTE: The DMG is the file format Apple Inc. uses for software distribution.

Build.txt

License.txt

Python.mpkg

ReadMe.txt

Before installing the program, take a moment to read the 'readme.txt' file to discover a lot, including that you may not just double click the installer 'Python.mpkg' because it's not signed by the Apple company (your gatekeeper settings will determine whether or not you can double click it: ***system preferences>>privacy and privacy>>general***). When you see a window after doing so, ignore it and move to the next step.

If your computer is using the gatekeeper default settings, just right click on the installer package and choose the option 'open with- installer.app' like the one below.

Having done that, you'll be taken through the standard installation. The subsequent steps are just the same as those under windows - no sweat!

Now that you have your program installed in your PC, we can now begin.

Introduction to Python: The fundamentals

In this chapter, I am going to introduce you to the following Python basics to help us in the subsequent chapters.

1. Keywords and Identifiers

2. Comments and statements

3. Datatypes

4. Python I/O and Import

5. Operators

6. Operator Precedence

Let's discuss these elements in detail:

The Python Keywords

Keywords are basically the list of words that the Python language has reserved for use in defining syntax and structure of the programming language. These words, for your info, are case sensitive.

The keywords, apart from False, None and True are in lowercase and you must write them like that. They include the following:

False	From	Yield
Finally	While	Elif
Return	Def	Or
Class	Nonlocal	Assert
Is	And	Import
None	Global	Else
For	With	Pass
Try	Del	Break
Continue	Not	In
Lambda	As	Except
True	If	Raise

Python Identifiers

In Python, an identifier is basically the name that's given to entities (or distinguishable objects) such as functions, class and variables. They help to differentiate entities.

Some rules of identifier writing

You can write an identifier by combining uppercase letters or lowercase letters, an underscore (_) or digits (0-9). For instance, *print_that_to*, *var_1* and *myClass* are valid identifiers.

You should not write an identifier beginning with a digit. For instance 1variable is wrong; variable1 on the other hand is correct.

You can use keywords as identifiers. Here is an example:

```
>>> global = 1
  File "<interactive input>", line 1
    global = 1
           ^

        SyntaxError: invalid syntax
```

Symbols like @, !, #, % etc cannot work in our identifier.

```
>>> a@ = 0
  File "<interactive input>", line 1
    a@ = 0
     ^

        SyntaxError: invalid syntax
```

Statements Indentation And Comments

Let's now discuss a bit about the Python statements, the reason why indentation is really important and usage of comments in Python programming.

Statement

Statements are the instructions that can be executed by a Python Interpreter. For instance a = 1 is an assignment statement. We have other kinds of statements such as *if*, *for* and *while*.

Multi-line statement

A newline character usually marks the end of a statement. We can however make a statement extend over many lines with the line prolongation character (\). For instance:

```
a = 1 + 2 + 3 + \
    4 + 5 + 6 + \
    7 + 8 + 9
```

Note that this is an explicit line continuation. Continuation is basically implied within the parentheses (), braces {} or brackets [] in Python. For example, we can implement the multi-line statement above as:

```
a = (1 + 2 + 3 +
     4 + 5 + 6 +
     7 + 8 + 9)
```

In this case, the parentheses do the line continuance implicitly. This is the same case with {} and []. For instance:

```
colors = ['red',
          'blue',
          'green']
```

You can also place multiple statements in one line by use of semicolons like this:

```
a = 1; c = 3
```

Indentation

Most languages like C++, java and C typically use braces to define a code block. Python on the other hand uses indentation. A code of block begins with indentation and finishes with the initial unindented line. It is up to you to determine the amount of indentation, but it's important to stay consistent throughout the block.

In general, we use four white spaces for indentation – which is widely preferred over tabs. Take a look at this example:

```
for i in range(1,11):
    print(i)
    if i == 5:
        break
```

In Python the indentation enforcement makes the code appear clean and neat. You will also note that this also results into programs that look consistent and similar.

You can ignore indentation in line continuation. However, it is recommended that you always indent so that your code is more readable. For instance:

```
if True:
    print('Hello')

    a = 5
```

-and

```
if True: print('Hello'); a = 5
```

While the two are valid and perform the same function, the former style is clearer.

NOTE: incorrect indentation results into indentation error.

Comments

While writing a program, you will also find comments extremely important. Comments describe all that is going on within a program so that when you are looking at the source code, you don't have a problem cracking it. It is possible to forget the essential details of the program you just wrote a month later; so it is always fruitful to explain these concepts in the form of comments.

Python only allows for the use of the symbol 'hash (#)' before writing a comment. This is spread out up to the newline character. All in all, programmers use comments to better understand a program.

NOTE: The comment is ignored by Python Interpreter.

```
#This is a comment
#print out Hello

print('Hello')
```

Multi-Line Comments

If you've got comments extending multiple lines, you can use the hash (#) at the beginning of every line. For instance:

```
#This is a long comment
#and it extends
#to multiple lines
```

Alternatively, you can use triple quotes which can be ' ' 'or " " ".

```
"""This is also a
perfect example of
multi-line comments"""
```

Python Variables And Types Of Data

Let's now discuss about variables, the rules of naming variables and the different types of variables you can make in Python.

Variables

A variable is the location in memory that is used to store some data or value. Variables are usually given unique names in order to distinguish between the memory locations. The rules of writing a variable name are similar to the rules for writing Python identifiers. You don't have to declare a variable before you use it. In Python, you just assign a value to a variable and it will exist. You don't even need to declare the variable type as this is handled internally based on the value type you assign to the variable.

Variable assignment

To assign values to a variable, you'll have to use the assignment operator (=). You can assign any value type to any valid variable.

```
a = 5
b = 3.2

c = "Hello"
```

You have three assignments here; **5** being an integer assigned to variable **a**. Likewise, 3.2 denotes a floating point number while 'Hello' is a string or sequence of characters that are assigned to the b and c variables respectively.

Multiple assignments

You can make multiple assignments in Python by using single statements like this:

```
a, b, c = 5, 3.2, "Hello"
```

If we want to assign the same value to multiple variables at once, we can do this as

```
x = y = z = "same"
```

This will assign the same string to all three variables.

Types of data in Python

In Python, each value contains a datatype and since everything in Python programming is an object, data types are essentially classes. Variables on the other hand are instance or object of these classes. Python contains various types of data types and some of the most important types include the following:

Numbers

Floating point numbers, integers and complex numbers fall under the category of Python numbers. In Python, they are defined as *float, int* and *complex class*. So that we're on the same page, let me talk about them briefly.

1. *Int/ or signed integers are the positive or negative whole numbers that don't contain a decimal point.*

2. *The float (also known as floating point real values) or floats typically represent numbers usually written with a decimal point that divides the integer and fractional parts. The floats may also assume a scientific notation, with e or E showing the power of 10 for instance, $2.5e2=2.5x10^2=250$.*

3. *The complex numbers assume the form a+ bJ in which a and b represent floats; the J is the square root of -1, an imaginary number. The real section of the number is a, and the imaginary part is b. However, complex numbers aren't used a lot in Python programming though.*

You can use the function 'type ()' to know which class a value or variable belongs to and the function 'isinstance ()' to check whether an object belongs to a specific class.

```
a = 5

print(a, "is of type", type(a))

a = 2.0

print(a, "is of type", type(a))

a = 1+2j

print(a, "is complex number?", isinstance(1+2j,complex))
```

Note the following:

- ✓ The integers can have any length- this, in any case, is only limited to the available memory.

- ✓ The accuracy of a floating number goes up to 15 decimal places. Decimal points separate floating numbers and floating points. 1 represents an integer while 1.0 is a floating point number.

- ✓ You write complex numbers in the form x+yj where x denotes the concrete part, and y denotes the imaginary part. Take a look at these examples:

```
>>> a = 1234567890123456789
>>> a
1234567890123456789
>>> b = 0.1234567890123456789
>>> b
0.12345678901234568
>>> c = 1+2j
>>> c

(1+2j)
```

Note the truncation of the float variable b.

Python Lists

We refer to the ordered sequence of items as lists. This is one of the most popular data types today, perhaps due to its flexibility. Note that all items in a list don't have to be of the same type. It's quite straightforward to declare a list. Items that are separated by commas are bounded by brackets [].

```
>>> a = [1, 2.2, 'python']
```

You can also utilize the slicing operator [] to extract a range of items or one item from the list. In Python, index begins from 0.

What's more, lists are typically mutable- the value of elements can be changed.

```
>>> a = [1,2,3]
>>> a[2]=4
>>> a
```

```
[1, 2, 4]
```

The Tuple

Just like a list, the Tuple is an ordered sequence of items. The difference comes in changeability- tuples are immutable; once you create them, you cannot modify them. We use tuples to write-protect data and are typically quicker than list since it can't change dynamically. It is always defined inside parentheses () where commas separate the items.

```
>>> t = (5,'program', 1+3j)
```

You can use the slicing operator

Note that you cannot change its value but you can use the slicing operator [] to extract items.

```
t = (5,'program', 1+3j)


# t[1] = 'program'
print("t[1] = ", t[1])


# t[0:3] = (5, 'program', (1+3j))
print("t[0:3] = ", t[0:3])


# Generates error

# Tuples are immutable

t[0] = 10
```

The others data types include strings, set and dictionary.

Strings are data types that represent textual data in computer programs which you can create using single, double or triple quotes. As you read, you'll discover that you can use escape sequences as you're working with strings. The escape sequences are basically the special characters having particular defined purpose when you use them within a string.

The sets are the unordered data collections that don't have any duplicate elements. A set will support operations such as intersection, difference or union – just like in Mathematics.

The dictionaries in Python are a group of key-value pairs and the elements it contains are indexed by keys. You will note that keys in a dictionaries have to be unique and so many other things. This owing to the importance of dictionary data type, many Python tutorials usually dedicate an entire chapter to the area. Don't skip it.

The Input, output and import

We'll now get to the two built-in functions: input () and print () to perform the task of I/O in Python. You'll also learn about the importation of modules and using them in your program.

Python gives many built-In functions which are always available to us at the Python prompt. Some of the functions such as print () and input () are used widely for the regular input and output operations respectively. Let's first take a look at the output section.

The Output using print () function

The print () function is mainly used to take data to the output device (screen).

Let's take an example:

```
print('This sentence is output to the screen')
```

```
# Output: This sentence is output to the screen
```

```
a = 5
```

```
print('The value of a is', a)
```

```
# Output: The value of a is 5
```

In the second statement on print (), you can see that there is a space between the value of variable 'a' and the string. While this is by default, we can change it.

The actual syntax of the print() function is:

```
print(*objects, sep=' ', end='\n', file=sys.stdout, flush=False)
```

The objects here are the values to be printed. The separator 'sep' used between the values defaults into a space character.

When all the values have been printed, 'end' is printed, and it defaults into a fresh line.

The object where the values are printed is 'The file' and 'sys.stdout' or the screen is its default value. This is a great example to illustrate this.

```
print(1,2,3,4)
```

Output: 1 2 3 4

```
print(1,2,3,4,sep='*')
```

Output: 1*2*3*4

```
print(1,2,3,4,sep='#',end='&')
```

Output: 1#2#3#4&

Output formatting

There are times when you will want to format your output to make it appear attractive. You can do this through the **str.format ()** technique. This technique is visible to all string objects.

```
>>> x = 5; y = 10
>>> print('The value of x is {} and y is {}'.format(x,y))
```

The value of x is 5 and y is 10

The curly braces '{}' here stand for placeholders. You can specify its printing order by making use of the numbers (tuple index).

```python
print('I love {o} and {1}'.format('bread','butter'))
# Output: I love bread and butter
```

```python
print('I love {1} and {o}'.format('bread','butter'))
# Output: I love butter and bread
```

In formatting the string, you can even make use of keyword arguments.

```python
>>> print('Hello {name}, {greeting}'.format(greeting = 'Goodmorning'
name = 'John'))
```

Hello John, Goodmorning

The Input

Our programs were static up until now. The variable values were hard coded or defined into the source code.

In order to ensure we have flexibility, it is important to get the input from the user. Python provides the ***input()*** function to make this possible. The input() syntax is:

input([prompt])

The prompt denotes the string you want displayed on the screen. This is largely optional though.

```python
>>> num = input('Enter a number: ')
Enter a number: 10
>>> num

'10'
```

You can see here that the value 10 is not a number but a string. In order to convert it into a number, you can use functions int() or float().

```
>>> int('10')
10
>>> float('10')

10.0
```

This very operation can be completed using the function **'eval()'**. It however takes it further. It is able to evaluate even expressions, but given the input is a string.

```
>>> int('2+3')
Traceback (most recent call last):
  File "<string>", line 301, in runcode
  File "<interactive input>", line 1, in <module>
ValueError: invalid literal for int() with base 10: '2+3'
>>> eval('2+3')

5
```

Python Import

As the program evolves, it's a prudent idea to break it into various modules. A module is a file that contains Python definitions and statements.

You can import the definitions within a module to another module or the Python interactive interpreter by using the 'import' keyword. For instance, you can type in 'import math' to import the 'math' module.

For example, we could import the math module by simply keying in import math.

```
import math

print(math.pi)
```

At this point, all the definitions within the 'math' module are accessible to us. We can also try importing a couple of attributes and functions only, by use of the 'from' keyword. For instance:

```
>>> from math import pi
>>> pi
3.141592653589793
```

Python will look at various places defined in **sys.path** while importing a module. This is a list of directory locations.

```
>>> import sys
>>> sys.path
['',
'C:\\Python33\\Lib\\idlelib',
'C:\\Windows\\system32\\python33.zip',
'C:\\Python33\\DLLs',
'C:\\Python33\\lib',
'C:\\Python33',
'C:\\Python33\\lib\\site-packages']
```

You can add your own location as well to this list. Please go through these examples to learn more about this:

Print Hello world!

Source code

```
# This program prints Hello, world!


print('Hello, world!')
```

The Output is

Hello, world!

Add Two Numbers

For the next one, I've used the arithmetic addition operator to combine the two numbers.

```
# This program adds two numbers


num1 = 1.5
num2 = 6.3


# Add two numbers
sum = float(num1) + float(num2)


# Display the sum
print('The sum of {0} and {1} is {2}'.format(num1, num2, sum))
```

The output is:

The sum of 1.5 and 6.3 is 7.8

You can change this operator to multiply, subtract, divide, floor divide (//) or even search for the remainder (%) of both numbers.

Source code: add two numbers given by the user

```
# Store input numbers
num1 = input('Enter first number: ')
num2 = input('Enter second number: ')

# Add two numbers
sum = float(num1) + float(num2)

# Display the sum
print('The sum of {0} and {1} is {2}'.format(num1, num2, sum))
```

The Output is

Enter first number: 1.5

Enter second number: 6.3

The sum of 1.5 and 6.3 is 7.8

Here, I asked the user to enter two numbers and the program displayed the sum of both numbers the user entered.

To take the input, I used the built in function input() . The input() returns a string, so that we convert it onto number by use of the float() function.

Alternatively, you can do this addition in one statement without applying any variables as follows:

```
print('The sum is %.1f' %(float(input('Enter first number:
'))+float(input('Enter second number: '))))
```

This program definitely doesn't use any variable (memory efficient) but it isn't really readable. There are people who find it hard to understand it. It is much better to write clear codes. Therefore, there is always some compromise between efficiency and clarity. You need to strike a balance.

The Python Operators

You will now learn all you need to know about the types of operators, their syntax and how you can use them.

Operators are the symbols in Python which are used to carry out logical or arithmetic computation. The operator operates on a value called the operand. For instance:

```
>>>2+3
```

```
5
```

In this example, + is the operator that does the addition while 3 and 2 are the operands and the output of the operation is 5.

There are a number of operators in Python. They include the following:

Arithmetic operators

Mathematical operations such as multiplication, subtraction and addition are performed by arithmetic operators.

Operator	Meaning	Example
+	Add two operands or unary plus	x + y +2
-	Subtract right operand from the left or unary minus	x - y -2
*	Multiply two operands	x * y
/	Divide left operand by the right one (always results into float)	x / y
%	Modulus - remainder of the division of left operand by the right	x % y (remainder of x/y)
//	Floor division - division that results into whole number adjusted to the left in the number line	x // y
**	Exponent - left operand raised to the power of right	x**y (x to the power y)

Let's take a look at some examples in this regard (python arithmetic operators):

Example #1

```
x = 15
y = 4


# Output: x + y = 19
print('x + y =',x+y)


# Output: x - y = 11
print('x - y =',x-y)


# Output: x * y = 60
print('x * y =',x*y)


# Output: x / y = 3.75
print('x / y =',x/y)


# Output: x // y = 3
print('x // y =',x//y)


# Output: x ** y = 50625
print('x ** y =',x**y)
```

This is the output you should expect when you run the program.

$$x + y = 19$$
$$x - y = 11$$
$$x * y = 60$$
$$x / y = 3.75$$
$$x // y = 3$$

$$x ** y = 50625$$

Comparison operators

When you want to compare values, you will use comparison operators. Depending on the condition, it either returns 'false' or 'true'.

Operator	Meaning	Example
>	Greater that - True if left operand is greater than the right	x > y
<	Less that - True if left operand is less than the right	x < y
==	Equal to - True if both operands are equal	x == y
!=	Not equal to - True if operands are not equal	x != y
>=	Greater than or equal to - True if left operand is greater than or equal to the right	x >= y
<=	Less than or equal to - True if left operand is less than or equal to the right	x <= y

Let's now go through a few examples of comparison operators in Python.

Example 2

x = 10

y = 12

Output: x > y is False

print('x > y is',x>y)

Output: x < y is True

print('x < y is',x<y)

Output: x == y is False

print('x == y is',x==y)

Output: x != y is True

print('x != y is',x!=y)

Output: x >= y is False

print('x >= y is',x>=y)

Output: x <= y is True

print('x <= y is',x<=y)

Logical operators

These include the not, or, and operators.

Operator	Meaning	Example
and	True if both the operands are true	x and y
or	True if either of the operands is true	x or y
not	True if operand is false (complements the operand)	not x

Let's take an example on the logical operators in Python.

Example 3

x = True

y = False

Output: x and y is False

print('x and y is',x and y)

Output: x or y is True

print('x or y is',x or y)

Output: not x is False

print('not x is',not x)

Bitwise operators

These operators act on operands as though they were binary digits strings. It operates bit by bit, hence the name. For instance, in binary, 2 is 10 & 7 is 111.

In this table, let y be 4 (0000 0100 in binary) and x be equal to 10 (0000 1010 in binary).

Operator	Meaning	Example
&	Bitwise AND	x& y = 0 (0000 0000)
|	Bitwise OR	x | y = 14 (0000 1110)
~	Bitwise NOT	~x = -11 (1111 0101)
^	Bitwise XOR	x ^ y = 14 (0000 1110)
>>	Bitwise right shift	x>> 2 = 2 (0000 0010)
<<	Bitwise left shift	x<< 2 = 40 (0010 1000)

It's about time we took the tutorial up a notch don't you think?

The Flow Control Using Python

You know the basics of instructions and how a program is a series of instructions and things like that – but programming is not limited to running one instruction after another. You have to appreciate that depending on the way the expressions evaluate, the program can decide to by-pass instructions, repeat some of them or choose either of them to run. Actually, most of us almost never want our programs to begin from the first line of code and execute every line all the way to the end. The flow control statements may decide the kind of instructions to execute under the particular conditions selected.

Flow control is also referred to as the process controlling the program execution sequence. We will discuss about control statements available in Python because it's very important to be able to control the program execution.

When you want to execute a code only if a particular condition is satisfied, decision making is required. Python programming uses *'if...elif...else'* statement when it comes to decision making.

If statement syntax

If test expression:

Statement(s)

What happens here is the program evaluates the 'test expression' and only executes the statement(s) if the test expression is true.

In the case the text expression is false, it won't execute the statement.

In Python, the 'if' statement body is shown by the indentation. The body begins with the indentation and the initial unindented line indicates the end. Python always interprets all non-zeros as true. None and 0 are taken to be false.

The if statement flowchart

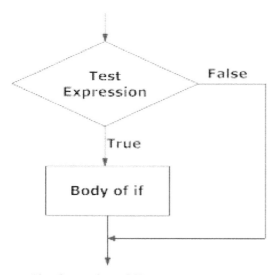

Fig: Operation of if statement

Let's have an example of if statement:

If the number is positive, we print an appropriate message

```python
num = 3
if num > 0:
    print(num, "is a positive number.")
print("This is always printed.")


num = -1
if num > 0:
    print(num, "is a positive number.")
print("This is also always printed.")
```

When you run it, the output to expect should be:

When you run the program, the output will be:

```
3 is a positive number
This is always printed
```

This is also always printed.

When you look at the example above, num> 0 is essentially the test expression. It's only when this evaluates to true that the body of 'if' is executed.

When variable num is = 3, test expression is true and the 'if' body is executed. On the other hand, if the variable num is =-1, the test expression is false and the 'if' body is automatically skipped.

The print() statement is executed irrespective of the test expression because it falls beyond the 'if' block (unindented).

The python if...else statement

The syntax of if...else

```
if test expression:
    Body of if
else:

    Body of else
```

If...else statement evaluates the 'test expression' and it's only when the test condition is true, that it executes the body. Conversely, when the condition is false, the body of else is executed. The blocks are separated by indentation.

The if...else flowchart

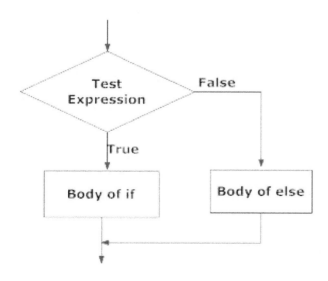

Fig: Operation of if...else statement

Let's take an example of if...else.

Program checks if the number is positive or negative

And displays an appropriate message

num = 3

Try these two variations as well.

num = -5

num = 0


```python
if num >= 0:
    print("Positive or Zero")
else:
    print("Negative number")
```


In the example above, when num is =3, it means the test expression is true and the 'if' body is executed while the 'else' body is skipped.

If the num is =-5, it means the test expression is false and thus, the 'else' body is executed and that of 'if' is skipped.

If num is =0, it means the test expression is true and the 'if' body is executed while that of 'else' is skipped.

The Python if...elif...else

The syntax of if...elif...else

```
if test expression:
    Body of if
elif test expression:
    Body of elif
else:

    Body of else
```

In case you're wondering, the **'elif'** is the short form for **else if**. It enables you to check for many expressions. In the case that all conditions are false, it turns to the condition of the next 'elif' block etc. When the condition is seen to be false, the else body is executed. Only a single block among the several if...elif...else blocks gets executed according to the condition. The 'if' block can contain one 'else' block alone- but it can also contain numerous elif blocks.

The flowchart of if...elif...else

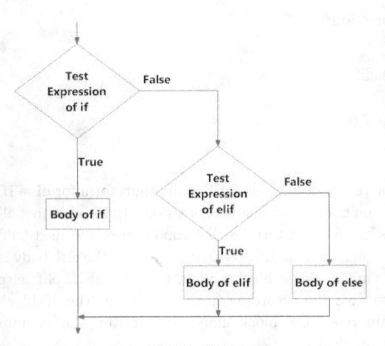

Fig: Operation of if...elif...else statement

58

Let's take an example of if...elif...else

```
# In this program,

# we check if the number is positive or

# negative or zero and

# display an appropriate message


num = 3.4


# Try these two variations as well:
# num = 0
# num = -4.5


if num > 0:
    print("Positive number")
elif num == 0:
    print("Zero")
else:
    print("Negative number")
```

When the num variable is positive, a positive number gets printed.

When the num variable is equal to zero, zero is printed.

When num variable is negative, a negative number is printed.

The nested if statements

You can also have an if...elif...else statement within another if...elif...else statement and this is referred to as nesting in computer programming.

All of these statements can be nested within one another and the only way to make out the level of nesting is through indentation. This can really get confusing so you should avoid it as much as you can.

Let's look at an example of nested if:

```
# In this program, we input a number
# check if the number is positive or
# negative or zero and display
# an appropriate message
# This time we use nested if

num = float(input("Enter a number: "))
if num >= 0:
   if num == 0:
      print("Zero")
   else:
      print("Positive number")
else:

   print("Negative number")
```

The first output:

Enter a number: 5

Positive number

The second output:

Enter a number: -1

Negative number

The third output:

Enter a number: 0

Zero

Python's for loop

We'll now discuss how you can iterate over a series of elements by use of the various variations of 'for loop'.

Python uses the 'for loop' to iterate over a series/sequence (list, tuple and string) or any other object that can be iterated. This process of iterating over sequences is known as *traversal*.

For loop Syntax

Syntax of for Loop

```
for val in sequence:

    Body of for
```

The 'val' as indicated above stands for a variable that assumes the value of an item within the sequence on each iteration. The loop continues until you get to the last item in the sequence. The body of for loop is separated from the other section of the code by the use of indentation.

The for loop flowchart

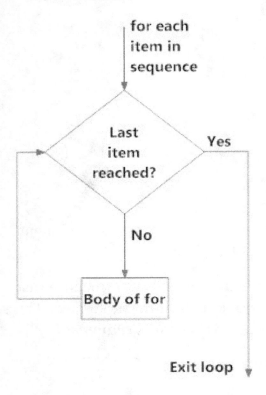

for each item in sequence

Last item reached?

Yes

No

Body of for

Exit loop

Fig: operation of for loop

Let's take an example.

```
# Program to find the sum of all numbers stored in a list

# List of numbers
numbers = [6, 5, 3, 8, 4, 2, 5, 4, 11]

# variable to store the sum
sum = 0

# iterate over the list
for val in numbers:
                sum = sum+val

# Output: The sum is 48
print("The sum is", sum)
```

When we run the program, the output should be:

The sum is 48

Range() function

You can create a sequence of numbers by using the range() function. Range (10) generates numbers starting from 0 to 9 (ten numbers).

You can also define the stop, start and step to be 'range(start, stop, step size)'. Step size defaults to 1 if it isn't provided.

NOTE: This function doesn't keep all the values in memory-thus, it would be rendered inefficient. Therefore, it remembers 'start, stop, step size' and creates the subsequent number on the go.

You can use the function 'list()' to force this function to give an output of all the items. Let me clarify that with an example:

```
# Output: range(o, 10)
print(range(10))

# Output: [0, 1, 2, 3, 4, 5, 6, 7, 8, 9]
print(list(range(10)))

# Output: [2, 3, 4, 5, 6, 7]
print(list(range(2, 8)))

# Output: [2, 5, 8, 11, 14, 17]

print(list(range(2, 20, 3)))
```

You can use the range() function in 'for loops' to iterate through a number sequence. You can combine it with the 'len()' function to iterate over a sequence by via indexing. Take a look at this example:

```
# Program to iterate through a list using indexing

genre = ['pop', 'rock', 'jazz']

# iterate over the list using index
for i in range(len(genre)):
    print("I like", genre[i])
```

By running the program, you'll be getting the following output:

```
I like pop
I like rock

I like jazz
```

For loop with else

A **for loop** can contain an optional block too. The else section will be executed if the items within the sequence use in for loop exhausts.

You can also use a break statement to stop a **for loop**. In this case though, the else part is ignored. Therefore, a **for loop's** else part will run if there's no break. Take a look at this example:

```python
digits = [0, 1, 5]


for i in digits:
    print(i)
else:
    print("No items left.")
```

When you run it, you will get the following output:

```
0
1
5
No items left.
```

The **for loop** in this case prints items of the list all the way until the loop depletes. When the **for loop** depletes/exhausts, it executes the code block in the else and prints the following:

No items left.

Well, that's just it for the for loop; let's now discuss the while loop:

While loop in Python

In programming, loops are used to repeat a particular block of code. In this chapter, you'll learn about the creation of a while loop in Python. In Python, the while loop is used to iterate over a code block provided the test expression/ or condition is true. In general, this loop is used when there is no understanding beforehand, of the number of times to iterate.

Python's syntax while loop

```
while test_expression:

    Body of while
```

In a while loop, you test the expression first and enter the body of the loop only if a 'test expression' actually evaluates to 'true'. Then after a single iteration, the test expression is checked once more, a process which goes on up until the 'test expression' evaluates to 'false'.

In Python, the while loop body is determined via indentation. The body begins with indentation and the first unindented line denotes the end. Any non-zero value is interpreted as true by Python, while none and zero are interpreted to be false.

While loop flowchart

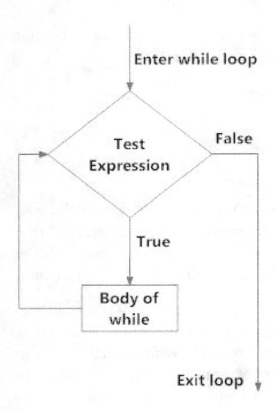

Fig: operation of while loop

Let's take a look at one example:

```
# Program to add natural
# numbers upto
# sum = 1+2+3+...+n

# To take input from the user,
# n = int(input("Enter n: "))

n = 10

# initialize sum and counter
sum = 0
i = 1

while i <= n:
    sum = sum + i
    i = i+1   # update counter

# print the sum
print("The sum is", sum)
```

You will get the following output when you run the program:

Enter n: 10

The sum is 55

In the program above, the test expression will be true provided i, the counter variable is either less than n or equal to n —this is 10 in the program.

We have to escalate the value of the counter variable in the loop's body as this is very important, even though it's usually forgotten. Failing to do this results in a never ending loop/infinite loop. The result is finally displayed.

Python while loop with else

Just like the one of for loop, it is optional to have an 'else' block with the while loop. If the condition in the while loop has evaluated to false, the 'else' part then executes. You can use a break statement to terminate the while loop (see next chapter). In this case, the 'else' part is ignored. Thus, a while else part of the while loop runs if there is no break occurring and the condition is false.

Take a look at this example:

```
# Example to illustrate
# the use of else statement
# with the while loop


counter = 0


while counter < 3:
    print("Inside loop")
    counter = counter + 1
else:
    print("Inside else")
```

The output

Inside loop
Inside loop
Inside loop
Inside else

In this case, we use a counter variable to print the 'inside loop' string thrice. On the final iteration, the while condition becomes 'false' and therefore, the 'else' section is executed.

Let's take another example:

Printing the Fibonacci sequence with python

In this example, we are going to be using while loop but your understanding of the python if...else statements is needed.

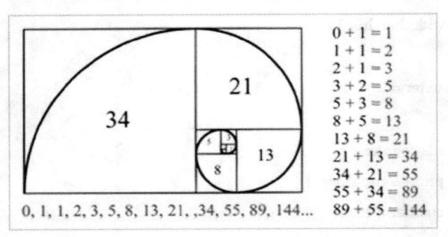

The Fibonacci sequence is basically the integer sequence of 0, 1, 1, 2, 3, 5... Apart from 0 and 1 which are the first two terms, all the other terms are gotten by adding the preceding two terms. Put simply, the nth term is obtained via the (n-1)th + (n-2)th term.

Source code follows on the next page.

```python
# Program to display the Fibonacci sequence up
provided by the user


# change this value for a different result

nterms = 10


# uncomment to take input from the user

#nterms = int(input("How many terms? "))


# first two terms

n1 = 0

n2 = 1

count = 0


# check if the number of terms is valid

if nterms <= 0:

   print("Please enter a positive integer")

elif nterms == 1:

   print("Fibonacci sequence upto",nterms,":")

   print(n1)

else:

   print("Fibonacci sequence upto",nterms,":")
```
73

Output

Fibonacci sequence upto 10 :
0, 1, 1, 2, 3, 5, 8, 13, 21, 34,

NOTE: In order to test this program, you can change the value of **nterms**. Here, we keep the number of terms in nterms. We set the first term to zero and the second one to 1. If the terms are more than 2, you can use the while loop to get the subsequent term in the sequence via the addition of the foregoing two terms. You can then swap the variables and go on with the process.

Let's now see how you can change the normal loop flow by using 'break and continue'.

Break And Continue In Python

In this chapter, you will learn about the use of break and continue statements to be able to alter the loop flow. This kind of statements can change the flow of a normal loop in Python.

Loops iterate over a code block 'til the test expression is false but at times, we wish to end the ongoing iteration or even the entire loop without looking at the test expression.

Take a look at these cases in which break and continue statements are used:

Break statement in Python

The break statement ends the loop that contains it. Just after the loop's body, the control of the program immediately flows to the statement. If the break statement is within a nested loop, or a loop within another, the break will end the deepest loop.

The break syntax

Break

Flowchart of break

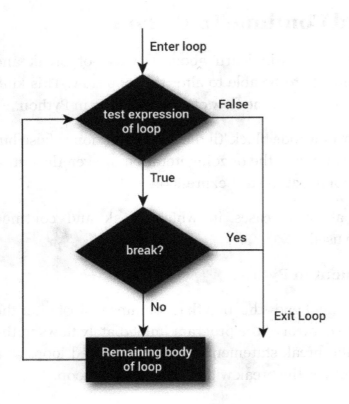

The operation of break statement in while loop and for loop is as follows:

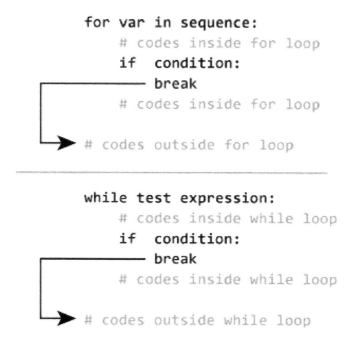

Let's have an example of the python break:

Use of break statement inside loop

```
for val in "string":
    if val == "i":
        break
    print(val)


print("The end")
```

The output is:

```
s
t
r
```

The end

Here, we iterate via the string sequence. We have to check whether the letter is 'i' to break from the loop. Thus, we notice in the output that all letters up to 'i' get printed and after that, the loop ends.

The Continue Statement

This kind of statement is used to jump the other part of the code within a loop only for the present iteration.

The continue syntax

Continue

Continue flowchart

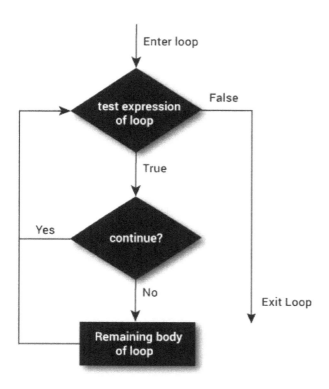

Take a look at the working of the continue statement in for loop and while loop:

```
for var in sequence:
    # codes inside for loop
    if condition:
        continue
    # codes inside for loop

# codes outside for loop
```

```
while test expression:
    # codes inside while loop
    if condition:
        continue
    # codes  inside while loop

# codes outside while loop
```

Example: Python continue

Program to show the use of continue statement inside loops

```
for val in "string":
    if val == "i":
        continue
    print(val)


print("The end")
```

The output is as follows:

```
s
t
r
n
g
The end
```

The program is just the same as the example above apart from the fact that you have to use continue to replace the break statement. If the string is 'i', we then continue with the loop, not exclusive of the rest of the block. As a result, we can see all the letters get printed except 'i'.

Congratulations for reaching this level. We have done many basic projects so far which are indeed the bases for larger projects. At this point, we need to look at others which are a little bit more solid, but apt for a diligent beginner like you.

Applying The Skills Learnt In Creating A Real Project With Python

Before you begin, you have to note the following:

Ensure you have PyCharm CE or Professional.

PyCharm is an integrated developmental environment (IDE) toolkit that we use to develop programs and build software in Python. If you don't already have it, please download it here (https://www.jetbrains.com/pycharm/download/#section=win dows) and follow the simple steps indicated to install it in your PC.

Today we'll be creating a simple python project with PyCharm. To get started with PyCharm, we'll first write a Python script. I'm sure you can recall the quadratic formula from your high school math .Well, also referred to as the A,B,C formula, we use the quadratic formula to solve simple quadratic equations : ax^2 +bx +c = o. Most of us find the manual method of solving quadratic formulae extremely dreary, so we are going to use a script instead.

NOTE: Pycharm suggests a number of project templates for the development of the different application types (Google AppEngine, Django etc). When Pycharm generates a new project from a project template, it gives out the corresponding structure of directory and specific files.

The process

Let's begin the project. On the welcome screen of Pycharm, click create new project. (if you had a project already open, you'd otherwise select file –New project).

Since we are going to create a simple script, select the Pure Python template – this creates an empty project for us. Choose the location of the project by clicking the browse button ⬚ beside the Location Field then specify your project's directory.

Important!

1. Selecting the kind of interpreter to use for any project is a very important decision. Python is a script language, meaning that a python interpreter converts your code. Since you can have different Python versions installed in your PC, and you have to select the one you would like for this particular project.

2. When you are using external libraries from anywhere, you have to manage their versions as well. The 'Pythonic' solution for this are virtualenvs which are sometimes abbreviated to venv. These basically help us keep the dependencies for our projects separate. While we are not going to use any dependencies for this project, it is always recommended to create a virtualenv for each new project we create, in case we want to add dependencies in future. To create a virtualenv, just click on this ⚙ icon and select create VirtualEnv. Specify the name of the virtual environment and location, and also the base interpreter.

Next, click create

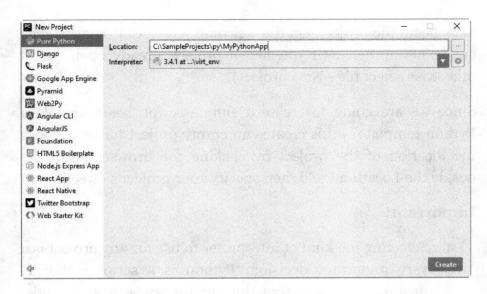

If you have a project open already, you'll be asked if you want to open a new project in the current window, after clicking create PyCharm. Select open in the current window- this closes the current project (but you will be able to reopen it later).

Create a python file

In the project tool window, choose a project root and press 'alt+insert':

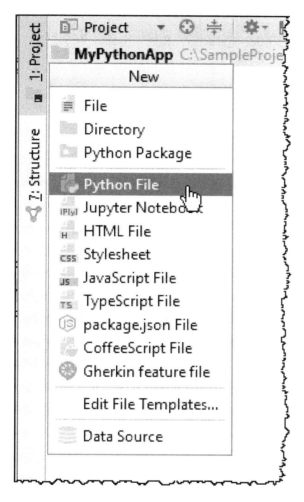

From the pop up window, select the option Python file and then type the file name 'solver'. PyCharm will create a Python file and open it for editing.

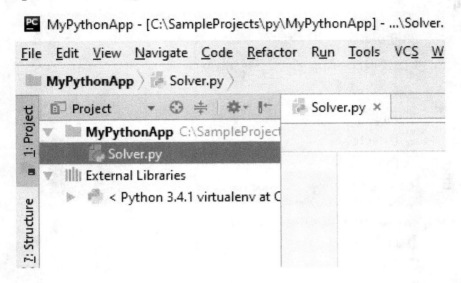

Edit the source code

Let's take a look at the Python file we have created. Just when you've began typing, you will notice that PyCharm is like a pair programmer since it looks over your shoulder and recommends how you should finish your line. For instance, you want to create a Python class. As you begin typing the keyword, a list of suggestions will appear.

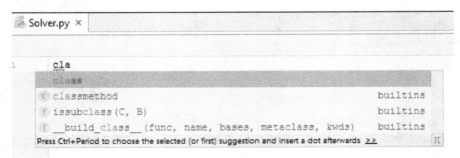

Select the keyword 'class' then type 'solver', the class name. The program instantly tells you about the missing colon, and the expected indentation.

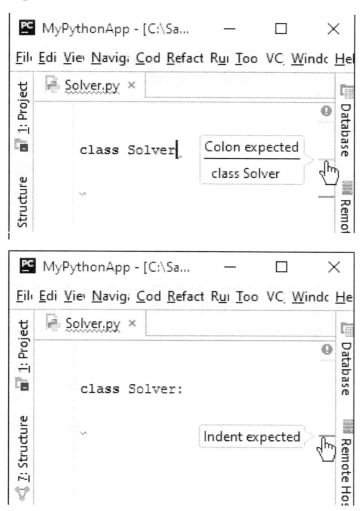

As you will notice, the error stripes in the right gutter. Just move your mouse pointer over an error stripe and PyCharm will show a balloon containing a detailed explanation. Since the program analyzes our code on-the-fly, you will see the results immediately in the inspection indicator (at the top of the right gutter). This indication works more like a traffic light where green indicates that everything is fine, and you can continue with your code. A yellow light on the other had means there are some minor problems which won't affect compilation but the red light means that there are some serious errors.

Let's go on and create the function 'demo': when you've just typed the opening brace, PyCarm will create the whole code construct and provide the proper indentation.

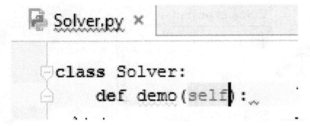

```
Solver.py ×

class Solver:
    def demo(self):
```

As you type, the unused symbols will grey out.

```
Solver.py ×

class Solver:
    def demo(self):
        a = int(input("a "))
        b = int(input("b "))
        c = int(input("c "))
```

When you've calculated a discriminant, they are rendered routinely. After that, look at the unresolved reference 'math'. PyCharm will underline it with the red line and show a red bulb.

When writing your code, it is at times recommended to modify your code constructs; here, PyCharm shows a yellow light bulb. Nonetheless, if PyCharm encounters an error, it shows the red light bulb. Whichever case may be, you can press alt+enter to display the suggestion list, which in this case, has a number of possible solutions.

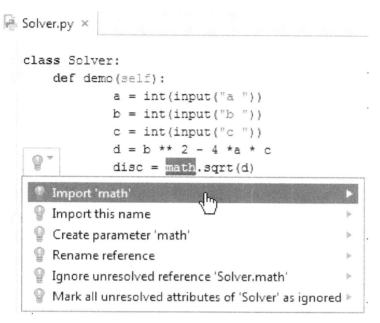

We'll now select importing the math library. The import statement will be added to the 'solver.py' file. After that, calculate the roots of the equation and then print them out. Finally, we'll call the function 'demo' of the class 'solver'.

```
import math class Solver: def demo(self): a = int(input("a ")) b =
int(input("b ")) c = int(input("c ")) d = b ** 2 - 4 * a * c disc = math.sqrt(d)
root1 = (-b + disc) / (2 * a) root2 = (-b - disc) / (2 * a) print(root1, root2)
Solver().demo()
```

Run the application

Next, right click on the editor and then on the context menu, select to run the 'Ctrl+Shift+F10' script. A console will be displayed in the run tool window. Let us try our code out by calculating the roots of the equation $3x^2 + 5x - 4$. In this case, enter a = 3, b= 5 and c= -4. The result should be:

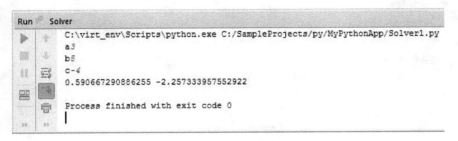

Debug configuration

When you run the script, PyCharm creates a temporary run or debug configuration for you. You should first save this configuration by scrolling to the run configuration dropdown on the top-right of your editor and selecting save configuration.

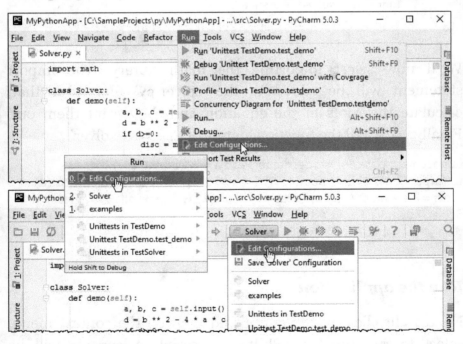

After that, select edit configurations to see what is happening.

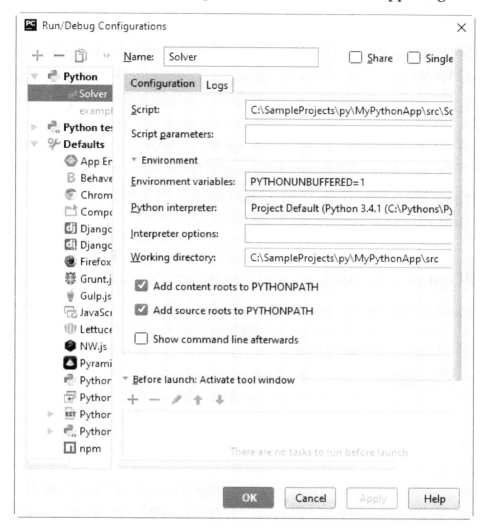

You need to realize there are various types of configuration for unit testing and the different frameworks such as Django in PyCharm Professional. If you would want to change how your program gets executed by PyCharm, you can configure various settings such as work directory, command line parameters and more here. For more details, you can take a look at run/debug configurations.

If you would want to use this Run configuration to begin the script, use this ▶ button beside the dropdown.

Congratulations! You have completed your first script in PyCharm.

Conclusion

We have come to the end of the book. Thank you for reading and congratulations for reading until the end.

I hope you have found the book insightful and practical as you start your journey to mastering python.

If you found the book valuable, can you recommend it to others?

One way to do that is to post a review on Amazon.

Thank you and good luck!

Arthur Keane

www.ingramcontent.com/pod-product-compliance
Lightning Source LLC
Chambersburg PA
CBHW061014050326
40689CB00012B/2641